Sabbath Season

A Call to Rest

Nichola Brown

© 2014 by Nichola Brown. All rights reserved.

No part of this publication may be reproduced, stored in a retrieval system, or transmitted in any way by any means, electronic, mechanical, photocopy, recording or otherwise without the prior permission of the author except as provided by USA copyright law.

Printed in the United States of America.

All Scripture quotations, unless otherwise indicated, are taken from the HOLY BIBLE, NEW INTERNATIONAL VERSION®. NIV® Copyright ©1973, 1978, 1984 by International Bible Society. Used by permission of Zondervan. All rights reserved.

Cover Design: SW Creatives, LLC

Published by SABBATH SEASON

To order copies of this book, visit our website:
www.sabbathseason.com

Library of Congress Control Number: 2014903600

ISBN 10: 0615958397

ISBN 13: 978-0-615-95839-2

1. Christianity 2. Christian Living 3. Self-Help

TABLE OF CONTENTS

Foreword 5

Dedication 8

Acknowledgments 9

Introduction 11

Chapter 1—Entering His Rest 15

Chapter 2—Harden Not Your Hearts 29

Chapter 3—Forgive Us Our Debts 41

Chapter 4—Healing for Your Soul 57

Chapter 5—Sabbath Delight 70

Chapter 6—God's Supernatural Provision 82

Chapter 7—Lessons from my Sabbath Season ... 91

Conclusion 103

References 110

Resources 111

About the Author 112

FOREWORD

The Bible makes it perfectly clear that human beings do not have the ability nor the capacity to fully understand God. "For my thoughts are not your thoughts, neither are your ways my ways," says the Lord. Some of the directives that God gives us seem difficult to comprehend and virtually impossible to carry out. For example, the commands to love our enemies and to pray for those who spitefully use and abuse us challenge us to our very core. However, some directives are literally *no-brainers*. The command to rest, for example, is one of God's mandates that really makes a lot of sense. We have experienced the physical lethargy, mental cloudiness, and emotional instability when we don't have a proper night's rest. Furthermore, we have experienced how compromised our immune system becomes when we fail to receive adequate rest. Most understand that rest is necessary for recuperation and restoration. However, the reality is that many (if not most) do not practice this divine mandate to rest. In fact, pharmaceutical companies who sell sleeping pills and companies who sell products with caffeine in them are profiting robustly off of our inability and/or refusal to rest.

To say it plainly, the world is in the midst of a major physical, emotional, and spiritual crisis. Stress is implicated in almost every one of the major diseases, whether physical

Sabbath Season

or psychological. Cases of anxiety and depression are skyrocketing, relationships are suffering, and productivity and efficiency is quickly dissipating. It does not matter what your profession is, you are not exempt. You can be the President of the United States; you can be a pastor; you can be a CEO of a Fortune 500 company; or a single-mother trying to juggle the world on your shoulders. We all need to rest!

To make this more personal, you who are reading this book are probably suffering from a severe case of *rest-deficiency*. Well, I have some great news. God has providentially led you to read this life-changing book, *Sabbath Season* by Nichola Brown. As a preacher of the gospel, pastoral counselor, and clinical psychologist, I have seen countless examples of people who are desperate for a real *Sabbath Season*. They are on the verge of suicide, a nervous breakdown, divorce, addiction, or pure psychosis because they have tried to fix their own lives without utilizing God's divine prescription to rest.

Nichola Brown, in the *Sabbath Season*, takes us along her personal journey to and through her season of rest, and gives jewels of wisdom that will undoubtedly transform your life. I say this not just because I have enjoyed reading this book; rather, I was one vessel that God used to bring her to and through her season of rest. I was her counselor and am now her life coach. I have witnessed the ups and downs; the unshakable faith and the drowning in fear; the laughter and the sobbing; the progress and the regress; the acceptance and the denial; and ultimately, I have witnessed

Foreword

God's transformative healing and restoration in concert with Nichola's surrender.

Now, Nichola Brown is a very effective disciple and licensed clinical social worker. Nichola courageously takes us along her personal journey where she surrendered and allowed the Holy Spirit to heal her of brokenness, to teach her how to forgive, and ultimately revealed to her how to walk worthily in her divine calling. My prayer is that you, like Nichola, will enter your *Sabbath Season* of rest!

God Bless You,

Dr. Jendayo K. Grady

DEDICATION

To my granny, mom

and

unborn children.

But the plans of the Lord stand firm, forever, the purposes of his heart through all generations. (Psalm 33:11)

ACKNOWLEDGMENTS

Thank you Abba, Father. You took every teardrop, every broken piece of my heart, and used it to give me an incredible gift, my purpose.

Thank you to my amazing mother. This book would not be possible without you. We have been through so much together; I praise God that he restored our relationship in ways that I could not have imagined. Thank you for your love and support.

Thank you to my spiritual family, who nurtured me with love. This was an incredibly challenging time in my life. However, God placed people in my life to encourage me along the way. A special thanks to my sister-friends: Veronica Carpenter, Yetunde Okesola, and Nique Wallace. Ladies, you may never truly know how much I appreciate your friendship, but I want you to know that your love, kindness, and compassion is something that I treasure in my heart.

God also placed spiritual moms and mentors in my life. Ms. Veronica, thank you for your prayers and encouragement. Thank you for believing in me. Colette, thank you for your friendship and for your support. Thank you to all the amazing women who God place in my life. They are too numerous to list, but God sees all that you do to comfort those around you.

Sabbath Season

Dr. Grady, thank you for encouraging me to write this book. I held this book deep in my heart, wrestling with whether or not to share it with the world. Thank you for your unwavering support.

Thank you to my church family at DC Regional Christian Church and our amazing Women's Ministry. I appreciate your commitment to teach the Word of God and to follow Jesus.

INTRODUCTION

What if God asked you to quit your job during one of the nation's worst economic crisis? Would you? For most of us, the answer is probably no. And like you, I would have said the same thing if God had not ultimately turned everything upside down in my life, causing me to make one of the hardest decisions I've ever had to face. That decision was to cease from work for a season to spend quality time in the presence of the Lord. God was calling me to enter a season of rest, a Sabbath Season, which eventually lasted for nine months. Crazy, I know!

In the American culture, taking time to rest is only acceptable if you are suffering from a major illness. And very few of us take our doctor's orders for respite seriously. In our society, resting is like a foreign concept; yet it is an important and necessary part of our lives. No one can live without it. Rest is not only vital to our physical well-being; it is also a divine part of God's plan that cannot be ignored. God created a weekly day of rest for man from the very beginning, which He called the Sabbath. In God's divine plan, observing and keeping the Sabbath was never meant to be optional or a dispensable part of society. Contrary to what many people assume, taking this day of rest was to demonstrate our dependence on Him. In other words, taking the time to cease from our labor allows us to worship God

Sabbath Season

for Who He is and for all He has done for us; however, over time, the practice of observing the Sabbath eroded from our culture and the complete opposite became the norm.

For the majority of people in our society, rest is viewed as expendable; people have learned to live their lives to the point of pushing themselves to the limit, ultimately living on as little rest as possible, often at the cost of their physical, emotional and spiritual well-being. The ability to access work twenty-four hours a day, seven days a week, overshadows the value of having a balanced life, which ought to contain elements of rest; and the results have been alarming. People are over-worked, stressed out, and overwhelmed. Families, including children, have experienced high levels of stress and anxiety, which has resulted in a complete burnout and breakdown for many. Once our weekends were used for relaxation and family-togetherness, now they have inevitably become just as busy as the weekdays. This is a factor found among many homes, including Christian households.

Although many Christians observe a version of the Sabbath by simply not working on Sunday, very few of us actually enter His rest. I'm not simply referring to a time where we do not work at our daily jobs; but I'm referring to a set time when we tune out the cares of this world, and enter an intimate place with Him. This is not because He needs it, but because we need it. We want to get to a position in our walk with God where He can call us at any time, and anywhere just to be with Him.

You may be looking at your schedule for the week and thinking that you don't have time to just rest. But God may call you to let go of some of your plans and choose to spend

Introduction

time with Him during the week. He wants to know if you're willing. He is asking all of His people to spend a few minutes a day in prayer and in the reading of the Word. You may find that at times He is calling on you to do certain things—whether it be turning off the music in the car while you drive or ceasing from eating that meal—just to talk to Him intimately. And you must have the faith to trust Him that entering into His rest, His presence, is what you need. Do you have the faith to believe that He is calling you? Do you have the trust to know that God is calling you to a season of rest?

In this book, *Sabbath Season*, I share with you the things that God revealed to me as I embarked on my Sabbath Season. During this period of resting with Him, He taught me the truth of His Word. He proved to me that His promise to always be my provider was real. He also gave me one of the things I needed most in order to continue living a godly life, and that was the healing of my soul. In doing so, God also exposed some things that I needed to deal with, areas such as doubt, un-forgiveness, pride, and an independent spirit that went contrary to His Word. God revealed to me that it was impossible to enter into the promises He had for me without first addressing these areas in my life. And God desires for each of us to enter into a land full of promises. However, it is possible to miss out on what God has in store for us because of our lack of faith and our unwillingness to take time and obey His command to rest and believe in Him. In this book I will share with you, based on the Word of God, how entering His rest and experiencing a Sabbath Season is necessary, if you will only believe.

Sabbath Season

If you will take hold of the instructions in God's Word, you will be able to enter a kind of Sabbath where you will learn how to hear and respond to the voice of God. You will learn that God is the creator of all things, and is able to create new things for you. You will learn to let go of your control and depend completely on God. You will learn that He is the source of all things, and that it is vital that you trust in His ability to provide for you. You will learn to trust His timing for the fulfillment of His promises in your life. During your Sabbath Season, God will demonstrate for you that He is able to make something out of nothing, and so much more.

Through this message, I want you to feel empowered and encouraged to take a step of faith to begin your own journey toward the Sabbath. As you read this book, which discloses some of my most vulnerable challenges, I hope that it gives you an opportunity to pray and reflect on your own lives and make decisions that God has been prompting you to make. I adamantly believe in what the writer states in Psalm 91:1, which reads, "Whoever dwells in the shelter of the Most High will **rest** in the shadow of the Almighty" (emphasis added). And now that the Holy Spirit dwells within Christians, we have the ability to live in this place of rest because we now walk by faith. May you be blessed as you take this journey into your Sabbath Season.

CHAPTER 1

Entering His Rest

God's promise of entering his rest still stands, so we ought to tremble with fear that some of you might fail to experience it. For this good news—that God has prepared this rest—has been announced to us just as it was to them. But it did them no good because they didn't share the faith of those who listened to God. For only we who believe can enter his rest (Hebrews 4:1–3, NLT).

It seems like none of us can ever get quite enough rest. How many times have we said, "There just aren't enough hours in the day"? We sometimes push ourselves physically to the point of exhaustion in order to meet all of our obligations. There are new studies, which come out annually, stating that Americans, especially, are sleep deprived; and the results of this can be costly. Recently, the Center for Disease Control (CDC) reported that insufficient sleep is a public epidemic.[1] But this need for rest is not just for the physical body, but for our spirit and soul as well. Although many of us understand the importance of rest,

---

[1] Center for Disease Control. 2014. Insufficient Sleep Is a Public Health Epidemic. (Last Modified January 14, 2014). http://www.cdc.gov/features/dssleep/ (assessed January 16, 2014).

few of us actually know how to attain this rest; but thanks be to God Who has given us the blueprint for finding this place of rest.

In the beginning, God described the need for man to rest, and demonstrated it after He created the world and the heavens. In Genesis, we read that God spoke the world into existence within six days, and

> By the seventh day God had finished the work he had been doing; so on the seventh day he rested from all his work. Then God blessed the seventh day and made it holy, because on it he rested from all the work of creating that he had done (Genesis 2:2–3).

This concept of resting from one's labor was so vital that even the Lord saw fit to set apart a day out of the week to enjoy the work of His hands. Now, we all know that God doesn't need to rest. He's God. In fact, the Scriptures read, "The Lord is the everlasting God, the Creator of the ends of the earth. He will not grow tired or weary" (Isaiah 40:28). Yet, He still set the pattern for His people in order to teach us how to set apart a sacred time to enjoy Him and His creation. In modern times, this could mean putting away our tools, our laptops, our phones, our anxious thoughts, and more, just to rest in His presence and glory. God wants us to enjoy His creation, not because we deserve this, but because He desires to bless us. This blessing comes from knowing that our total confidence and assurance for all our needs is in Him.

Entering His Rest

As God began to manifest Himself to mankind, He gave us the instruction to enter into a time of rest in which we cease from our works to enjoy all that He has done for us. We further learn about the importance of rest through our study of the children of Israel. God cares about our rest and expected that His children observed the Sabbath, which is reflected in the Word.

He Created a Pattern

The Hebrew word for rest is Shabbat, which means, stopping or ceasing. During biblical times, the Israelites were to observe the Shabbat or Sabbath, celebrating it for generations to come as a lasting covenant (Exodus 31:16). From what we read, the principle was also observed in different cycles or events, such as the seventh day of the week, the seventh year (also called the Sabbath Year), and the observance of the Year of Jubilee, which occurred after seven full Sabbath Years. Presently, many orthodox Jews strictly observe these traditions. During the Shabbat, they are expected to spend time with God, singing, praying, and reading His Word. They also use this time to enjoy their families and communities. There is an understanding among them that by maintaining the Shabbat, they have been able to remember an important aspect of their faith. However, this blessed principle remains available to everyone who believes.

Growing up as a believer for over fourteen years, my understanding of the Sabbath was limited and I never attempted an in-depth Bible study through my walk. While I knew that the Sabbath was mentioned in the Scriptures, I

Sabbath Season

did not see how relevant it was to me, especially as a New Testament Christian. I knew that the Sabbath was the day that God rested from His work; I also knew that observing the Sabbath was a part of the Ten Commandments; but I didn't see how it was relevant to me. For many Christians today, observing the Sabbath occurs on Sundays and not Saturdays as it is with most orthodox Jews; and I understood that not going to work and attending church on Sundays was our way of honoring the Sabbath. But I did not come to realize how to properly apply this concept to my life. Most of the time, my Sundays were just as busy as any other day. I would pile on activities and events on this day just as I did during the work week. This day became like every other day, overscheduled. As a result, I found myself completely exhausted and anxious about the upcoming workweek, because I had little time to rest. After experiencing this multiple times, I began reading the Scriptures, and it became clear to me that God's Word concerning honoring a day of rest was still relevant in today's time. As the Scriptures read,

> Remember the Sabbath day by keeping it holy. Six days you shall labor and do all your work, but the seventh day is a Sabbath to the Lord your God. On it you shall not do any work, neither you, nor your son or daughter, nor your male or female servant, nor your animals, nor any foreigner residing in your towns. For in six days the Lord made the heavens and the earth, the sea, and all that is in them, but he rested on the seventh day. Therefore the Lord blessed the Sabbath day and made it holy (Exodus 20:8–11).

Entering His Rest

While some people may not find this passage applicable to their lives, I know that God prompted me to cease for a season and to learn the proper balance. He wanted to show me that observing and honoring a time of Sabbath was not only for the children of Israel in the times of old, but also for me and others today. He wanted to teach me that resting was essential for every individual because it allowed us to heal, not only in our bodies, but also in our spirit and soul. As a being composed of three parts (body, spirit, and soul), it was important that I took time out of my hectic schedule to rest from my weekly labor, and soon I would learn to rest from my emotional labor. I quickly learned that a time of Sabbath offers something that many of us are desperately in search of: rest for our body, spirit, and soul.

Rest for Your Body

> "In vain you rise early and stay up late, toiling for food to eat—for he grants sleep to those he loves" (Psalm 127:2).

According to the American Heart Association, heart disease is the leading killer of Americans and the number one killer of women in America. A contributing factor in heart disease is stress. Stress can lead to hypertension, asthma, ulcers, sleep disturbance, anxiety, depression, overeating, and so on. Stress is meant to be a signal to our bodies to respond to danger, causing us to respond with "fight or flight." Although this is meant to be a temporary condition, many of us live with chronic stress for weeks, months, and years.

Sabbath Season

We are unwilling and unable to cope with the stress in our lives. We are unwilling to let go of the grip we have on our lives, our plans, our schedules, and our careers. As a result, we are dying physically, emotionally, and spiritually because we are disobeying God. This impacts our entire being. Some people are literally working themselves to death.

The National Highway Traffic Safety Administration roughly estimates that 100,000 police-reported crashes are due to driver fatigue each year, resulting in around 1,550 deaths, 71,000 injuries, and $12.5 billion in monetary losses.[2] Studies show a high correlation between the mortality rate and lack of rest. These factors are not only alarming, but are direct results of our unwillingness to apply God's instructions for literally observing a time of Sabbath.

Without physical rest or sleep, no one is able to function. While we may set goals for ourselves, which entail the completion of projects, we must listen to our bodies when they tell us that it is time to rest. Even the Lord did not complete His creation in one day, but took the time (six days) to make the world exactly as He saw fit. More importantly, we can observe that not only did the Lord rest on the seventh day, but also ceased from completing a particular project each day, only to resume work again the next day.

In our culture, we attempt to use various methods in order to avoid sleep or physical rest; but there is not enough coffee in the world that will keep us moving non-stop. On average, it is estimated that eight to nine hours of rest is good

---

[2]National Sleep Foundation. 2014. Facts or Stats. http://drowsydriving.org/about/facts-and-stats/ (accessed January 16, 2014).

enough to help us function properly throughout the day, and this is a factor we must consider. Although the challenges of life force us to think that we must utilize every hour of the day to accomplish our tasks, we must give special care to resting our bodies, especially for us women.

As I consider my own struggles and obstacles, I am amazed at the accomplishments that women have achieved, especially those who are mothers. For most of these women, working full-time jobs and supporting the needs of their families is a priority to their individual needs. But I want to take a moment and encourage these women because it is imperative that they find the time to incorporate rest and relaxation in their lifestyle. For people in general, resting our bodies allows us to find rest in our other components, especially in our spirit and soul.

Rest for Your Spirit

> "The Spirit himself testifies with our spirit that we are God's children. Now if we are children, then we are heirs—heirs of God and co-heirs with Christ, if indeed we share in his sufferings in order that we may also share in his glory" (Romans 8:16–17).

Many of us find it difficult to set our spirit at rest. This is because a prerequisite for finding this spiritual rest is putting our faith in Jesus Christ alone for our salvation. Think about it, a person who is drowning never truly finds rest until they are rescued and delivered to safe ground. Until someone comes to save us, we are expending all of our energy trying to stay afloat. Often times, this reflects our spiritual condition when we do not put our faith in Christ, alone. Jesus is our Savior. He rescues us from what Peter refers to as our empty way of life (1 Peter 1:18). We are delivered by the perfect work of the Son. His perfect life, suffering, death, burial, and resurrection represents the full payment required, in order for us to have the ability to enter His eternal rest. After suffering on the cross, "Jesus said, 'It is finished.' With that, he bowed his head and gave up his spirit" (John 19:30). Jesus committed His spirit into the hands of His Father and we can also commit our spirit into the hands of Jesus. Because of what He endured on the cross for us, we can rest in His healing (Isaiah 53:5).

In order to attain this spiritual rest, we must take time to reflect and meditate on the power of God's Word. God uses the concept of the Sabbath to get us to put our faith and trust entirely in Christ. Honoring this time puts us in a place of total rest and security in Him.

Rest for Your Soul

"My soul rests in God alone" (Psalm 62:1, WEB).

Our soul is also in need of rest. We are all seeking something that will bring us peace, and God is the only one Who can give us this kind of rest and peace. It can be found in no one else. This is a profound statement that we must all take to heart.

At times, there will be things that will deeply trouble our soul. Often times, we may look to our career, relationships

Entering His Rest

with others, or other external connections to find a sense of peace and comfort. But the Lord would say to us,

> Come to me, all you who are weary and burdened, and I will give you rest. Take my yoke upon you and learn from me, for I am gentle and humble in heart, and you will find rest for your souls (Matthew 11:28–29).

God wants us to bring those things that overwhelm us and stress us to Him so that He can handle them as He sees fit. There is nothing too hard for the Lord, and we must have the faith to believe that we can bring Him our most painful and worrisome experiences "because He cares for you" (1 Peter 5:7). When we observe a time of Sabbath, we learn to take off the cares of this world and put on His yoke. God wants all of His children to find rest for their souls, and what an incredible witness that is to the world. What a witness it will be when people can see that in spite of our trials and tribulations, we do not respond frantically or in fear because our soul has found rest in the Lord! People will come to us to inquire about this peace that passes all understanding.

A Modern-Day Sabbath

> "My presence will go with you, and I will give you rest" (Exodus 33:14).

Although the concept of the Sabbath is an Old Testament commandment, it gives us clear instructions for how to enjoy this life that God has given us. As Christians, we have the opportunity to restore the biblical principles of rest and not conform to the patterns of this world. As the world seems to get busier and busier, we Christians can return to the principles that keep us grounded to the source and the creator of everything.

So what can "Entering His Rest" look like in a modern world? In Matthew 28, Jesus says to "Come to Him." We need to consistently choose to set aside time to go and connect with Him. We begin this journey by making God a priority in our lives and in our schedules. He desires to know that we value Him over everything and everyone, and this can be demonstrated in how we choose to spend our time. For a long time, I did not know how this looked. But I discovered ways in which God was calling me to observe the Sabbath. First, I began by setting aside time, not just my quiet time, but time to really study and read the Word of God. So my personal Sabbath began with digging deeper into the Scriptures. Secondly, I began to go to God with the things that hurt my heart and soul. I learned that confessing my faults and pains to Him brought about great healing to me. Thirdly, I began to see that honoring the Sabbath meant disconnecting from the world and spiritually connecting with God for a period of time. The Sabbath is a time when God can speak to us about His plans for our lives. However, if we are distracted we will not hear His voice. God desires to reveal things about Himself to us. During my Sabbath, I rarely watched television or listened to secular music. I also limited my time on the Internet, especially social media. For me, I would often use those things as distractions to not fully address the problems I had. But I needed to learn how

Entering His Rest

to quiet my mind, and be present with the Lord in order to tackle the challenges that I felt were too overwhelming for me.

As you consider ways of implementing your own Sabbath Season, know that it will look differently for you than it did for me. But you must remember that the most important thing is that you set aside the time necessary to enter into His rest, for that time is holy. And when you do, you will quickly see that all your needs are met because you have learned to put your trust in Him.

Sabbath Season

Sabbath Reflection

1. Are you in a season of frantic distraction? (Describe)

   _____
   _____
   _____
   _____
   _____
   _____
   _____
   _____
   _____
   _____
   _____
   _____

2. Do you need rest? (Describe) _____

   _____
   _____
   _____
   _____
   _____
   _____
   _____

Entering His Rest

3. Do you believe that God will pull you through though it seems the worst time to slow down?

Sabbath Season

4. Is your faith being tested? If so, in what way(s)?

CHAPTER 2

Harden Not Your Hearts

"So, as the Holy Spirit says: 'Today, if you hear his voice, do not harden your hearts as you did in the rebellion, during the time of testing in the wilderness'" (Hebrews 3:7–8).

"Let us, therefore, make every effort to enter that rest, so that no one will perish by following their example of disobedience" (Hebrews 4:11).

Story of the Israelites

> Therefore since it still remains for some to enter that rest, and since those who formerly had the good news proclaimed to them did not go in because of their disobedience, God again set a certain day, calling it 'Today.' This he did when a long time later he spoke through David, as in the passage already quoted: 'Today, if you hear his voice, do not harden your hearts' (Hebrews 4:6–7).

The story of the Israelites' wilderness experience is rich with lessons on the importance of entering into the rest of God. What was supposed to be an eleven-day journey toward entering the Land of Promise quickly became a forty-year voyage. Their decision to not have faith in God ultimately had a generational impact. The example of the Israelites wandering in the desert for forty years illustrates the truth about rebellion against God. (Read Numbers 13–14:1–39 to understand how faithlessness can have lasting consequences on God's people.) God eventually gave the Israelites the land because of a promise he made to Abraham, Isaac, and Jacob; but the first generation did not inherit it because of their doubt and unbelief. Nevertheless, it was the faith of Abraham that allowed for future generations to enter into a land that God wanted for them.

The story of the Israelites' wilderness experience is extraordinary. When they arrived at Kadesh, a place that was close to their final destination, the Israelites sent twelve spies to survey the land and confirm that God's promise was real. God gave the Israelites clear, but nonspecific instructions on how to take possession of this land. He did not include details on how this would be accomplished, but He expected them to trust that He would deliver them just as He had done before. During their enslavement, God performed numerous miracles in order to bring them out of Egypt. The Israelites saw God part the Red Sea, allowing them to cross on dried land. When their Egyptian enemies tried to pursue them, God caused the waters to overtake them. Time and time again, God demonstrated His power and authority for the Israelites.

For a long time, I couldn't understand how the Israelites could doubt God, especially when He had given them so much evidence of His power and provisions. However, I didn't have to think too hard to realize that I was just like the Israelites. Have you ever doubted God right after He performed a miracle right in front of your face? Well, I have. For example, in writing this book, I must say there was constant doubt and fear that I battled daily. Although God gave me instructions to complete this book, my doubts and fears quickly surfaced. What we must understand is that our trepidations can prevent us from reaching the place that God has commanded us to take possession of. He doesn't have to say exactly how we are to do it; He just said it was ours to take possession of.

God is gracious and gives each of us an opportunity to respond to His instructions; He wants us to avoid the consequences of our forefather's faithlessness by trusting that He will provide all things that we need, thereby entering His rest. Each of us must respond to the call on our lives. Always remember, "Today, if you hear his voice…." God is so patient with us and he wants us to enter into the special place to find rest for our soul. Is God calling you to enter his rest today?

Children of the Wilderness

I sometimes wonder what it was like for the second generation of Israelites who lived in the desert. Besides the fact that God was waiting until the people from that generation died off, what was life like for them? Can you imagine? Instead of playing and eating in the lush gardens promised to them, they were kicking around sand and eating the same meal every day for forty years. But they

Sabbath Season

also witnessed the daily miracle of manna falling from the sky, and the double portions on the sixth day of the week in order to observe the Sabbath. Many of them probably heard the stories of how their lives were in Egypt, and then about the miraculous events that took place in order to get their families out of Egypt. Some of them may have even remembered seeing these miracles themselves. However, they were now wandering in the desert because their parents disobeyed God. And they were paying for a decision their parents made.

After disobeying God's instructions to enter the Promised Land, God asked Moses, "How long will these people treat me with contempt? How long will they refuse to believe in me, in spite of all the signs I have performed among them?" (Numbers 14:11). God barred the spirit of the faithless to enter into His promised rest. When God saw their lack of faith, He told them,

> 'Not a man of this evil generation shall see the good land I swore to give your forefathers, except Caleb son of Jephunneh. He will see it, and I will give him and his descendants the land he set his feet on, because he followed the Lord wholeheartedly' (Deuteronomy 1:35–36).

So, how do you think their parents handled not entering the Promised Land? Were they bitter? Did they admit that it was a mistake? Did they try to teach their children to have faith? Did it drive them to repentance? Despite the lack of faith of the parents, as we can see from the Scriptures in Ezekiel, God wanted to give the next generation the opportunity to inherit what their parents abandoned. "I said to their children in the wilderness,

> 'Do not follow the statutes of your parents or keep their laws or defile yourselves with their idols. I am the Lord your God; follow my decrees and be careful to keep my laws. Keep my Sabbaths holy, that they may be a sign between us. Then you will know that I am the Lord your God' (Ezekiel 20:18–20).

He warned the children of the desert not to follow their parents. And as a result, God was able to bless future generations because of their faith.

> For you know that God paid a ransom to save you from the empty life you inherited from your ancestors. And the ransom he paid was not mere gold or silver. It was the precious blood of Christ, the sinless, spotless Lamb of God. God chose him as your ransom long before the world began, but he now revealed him to you in these last days (1 Peter 1:18–20, NLT).

As Christians we must take possession of the inheritance, which comes from God.

Modern-day Wilderness

The wilderness is a reflection of a type of spiritual journey that takes place in our lives. God has called all of us to enter His spiritual rest. However, what God intends

Sabbath Season

to only take eleven days, for many of us, it will take forty years to get there because of our lack of faith. Many of us are children of modern-day wildernesses with our own desert experience. But God has a plan for us to enter His rest today, if we do not harden our hearts. I was unaware of the importance of my faith to receive the things God had promised me. And I had to learn that the promises of God are given to me by faith (Romans 4:16). We have to be able to believe in God and in His promise before we can receive them. God wants to take us out of this dry place and perform miracles in our lives. However, we must be willing to believe Him and let go of our past experiences. These experiences may include broken relationships, bitterness, un-forgiveness and faithlessness. We must recognize when we are in a wilderness and trust God to bring us out and into His Land of Promise and rest, for as the New Testament reveals, God reminds the Christians to not harden their hearts, but to believe in God in order to enter into His rest.

Cost of Unrest

> If after all this you will not listen to me, I will punish you for your sins seven times over. I will break down your stubborn pride and make the sky above you like iron and the ground beneath you like bronze. Your strength will be spent in vain, because your soil will not yield its crops, nor will the trees of your land yield their fruit (Leviticus 26:18-20).

God takes our disobedience and faithlessness seriously. One of the biggest areas in which God confronts us is in the area of pride. If we are unwilling to be humble, to listen, and to follow His instructions, He will allow us to fall because of our pride. How many of us have experienced this? We have gone outside of God's will and disobeyed His direction for us, only to later experience the consequences. I have done this in my own life, with career choices and dating relationships. I listened to and trusted myself rather than the prompting of the Holy Spirit, and the results were always devastating. I experienced painful break ups, and I quickly learned that there were physical, emotional, and spiritual consequences for rebelling against God's will. And when we are out of the will of God, we may do things to try and distract us from addressing this sin, which further causes us to experience unrest. Many of us are drifting around in our own spiritual wilderness; and although God is still with us, we are not living in the abundant blessing of God, because we do not have the faith to enter into the spiritual Promise Land God has prepared for us.

For years, I knew God wanted me to deal with my "wilderness experience," particularly the broken relationship with my mother. However, I did not want to confront the pain that I buried deep in my heart. Instead of addressing the pain, I ran away from it. In fact, I sprinted away. I figured that if I kept myself busy, I wouldn't have time to feel how much my heart was broken. I buried it with school, taking on different jobs, pursuing professional goals, entering dating relationships, and just about anything else I could find to distract me. I was doing exactly what Jonah did when he tried to run away from God. But God was persistently asking me to address the issue with my mother. And I was consistently avoiding it. At some point, I did agree to enter therapy in order to start the healing process; but in 2008, I dropped it because I did not want to confront the pain. Instead, I chose to enter a dating relationship in hopes that it would heal my soul.

The gentleman and I dated for several years and even talked about marriage; however, in the back of my mind, God told me to let go of the relationship. What a terrifying thing to hear from God when you're in a relationship with someone you love. I tried to ignore it. I prayed about it, but I knew in my heart of hearts that God did not want me in this relationship. I had so much that I needed to work on, so much that I needed to change. Letting go of the relationship was painful and difficult, but it was something I knew God told me to do. I wasn't sure why, but later I realized that God wanted access to my heart. But as long as I had idols in my heart, He could not be in His rightful place in my life. I spent years going around the issues that I knew needed addressing in my life. So in 2011, when I began counseling again, I knew that it was time to confront this head-on and not run away or try to busy myself once again. The result of this obedience has led to an abundance of healing and restoration, especially between me and my mother.

A Different Spirit

> But because my servant Caleb has a different spirit and follows me wholeheartedly, I will bring him into the land he went to, and his descendants will inherit it (Numbers 14:24).

Harden Not Your Heart

God is calling us to be like Caleb and Joshua in our generation. The difference between them and the first generation of wilderness wanderers was their faith to believe that God would perform His promise to them. Their faith allowed them to believe God's words and not concede their inheritance to the giants in front of them. God prevented the Israelites of that generation from ever entering the Promised Land. As we learned from reading the Scriptures, this generation died in the wilderness; nevertheless they experienced some of God's provisions, but never His full blessings. We must strive to be like Caleb and Joshua so that we can experience the fullness of God's grace and inevitably enter a time where God's rest is for our own lives. Like them, we must carry a "different spirit," and demonstrate to the world that not only are we willing to address the hardships in our lives, but we are confident in knowing that when we fulfill the will of God and obey His instructions, we will find supernatural rest for our souls.

Sabbath Season

Sabbath Reflection

1. Review Numbers 13 & 14:1-39. Caleb and Joshua entered into the Promised Land because they had a "different spirit" among the religious leaders of their generation. Describe what it means to have a "different spirit" in your generation.

   _____
   _____
   _____
   _____
   _____
   _____
   _____
   _____
   _____
   _____
   _____
   _____
   _____

2. In what way(s), are you a child of the spiritual wilderness? (Describe) _____

   _____
   _____
   _____

Harden Not Your Heart

3. Are you currently living in a spiritual wilderness or in the Promised Land?

Sabbath Season

4. What spiritual legacy will you leave the next generation?

CHAPTER 3

Forgive Us Our Debts

"And forgive us our debts, as we also have forgiven our debtors" (Matthew 6:12).

Now that you have an understanding what is meant by the Sabbath and how God uses it to cause us to reflect on and rest in Him, I want to share with you many of the lessons I learned as a result of entering a time of Sabbath, a period that lasted for nine months. A major lesson was learning how to forgive those that had done me wrong, even the people that were closest to me.

To begin, I want to compare my experience with that of the forgiveness of financial debt. Have you ever paid off a large bill or paid off your car? It feels as though a weight has been removed, literally. You are no longer burdened with the obligation to pay that debt. I experienced that feeling after making my final car payment a few years ago. Once the loan was paid off, there was a great sense of freedom. It was an amazing feeling to no longer have that obligation to make to the lender. But imagine if someone decided to pay this debt for you. There would be an incredible sense of gratitude.

Sabbath Season

As Christians, we all know what this feels like. We owe God our lives because of our sin; however, instead of paying the debt we owe Him for the cost of our sin, Jesus paid the debt. This is the ultimate debt forgiveness. The Maker of the Universe, who required my life for the sins I have committed here on earth, let me walk away with a new life once I accepted Jesus as my Savior. And instead of receiving a death sentence, it's like Jesus stepped in and said, "I will take the punishment that was meant for you. I will pay for your sins with my life." How incredible is that feeling? I get to walk out of the courthouse, free as a bird. Now the question is: how will I live?

During my Sabbath Season, God taught me that the same way He released forgiveness to me was the same way I needed to forgive the debts of others. And during your time of Sabbath, God will empower you and grant you the opportunity to impart this experience to other believers, enabling you to release and forgive others from their debts. We have an opportunity to imitate Christ, for as Jesus said in Matthew 10:8, "Freely you received; freely give." What if we put this into practice? What if we forgive all the debt that others owed us?

In my study of the Sabbath Year in particular, during the Year of Release or the Year of Cancelling Debt, which took place every seventh year, God asked His people to cancel the debt owed to them. Let's read Deuteronomy 15:1–11.

> At the end of every seven years you must cancel debts. This is how it is to be done:

Forgive Us Our Debts

Every creditor shall cancel any loan they have made to a fellow Israelite. They shall not require payment from anyone among their own people, because the Lord's time for canceling debts has been proclaimed. You may require payment from a foreigner, but you must cancel any debt your fellow Israelite owes you. However, there need be no poor people among you, for in the land the Lord your God is giving you to possess as your inheritance, he will richly bless you, if only you fully obey the Lord your God and are careful to follow all these commands I am giving you today. For the Lord your God will bless you as he has promised, and you will lend to many nations but will borrow from none. You will rule over many nations but none will rule over you. If anyone is poor among your fellow Israelites in any of the towns of the land the Lord your God is giving you, do not be hardhearted or tightfisted toward them. Rather, be openhanded and freely lend them whatever they need. Be careful not to harbor this wicked thought: 'The seventh year, the year for canceling debts, is near,' so that you do not show ill will toward the needy among your fellow Israelites and give them nothing. They may then appeal to the Lord against you, and you will be found guilty of sin. Give generously to them and do so without a grudging heart; then because of this the Lord your God will bless you in all your work and in everything you put your hand to. There will always be poor people in the land. Therefore I command you to be openhanded toward your fellow Israelites who are poor and needy in your land.

Sabbath Season

The Sabbath Season is a time where we remember to release and let go of the things that hold us captive and take care of the needy. This concept is not exclusive to monetary debt, but it relates to emotional debt as well. As I reflected on the debt I needed to cancel, it became very clear to me that the primary debt I needed to cancel was the debt I believed that my mother owed me. I held a large bill in my heart against my mother and father for the painful things I endured in my childhood. I carried around an emotional ledger in my heart. With each negative interaction I had with her, I would immediately place a charge against her account. During my Sabbath Year, I began to learn how to start the process of forgiving that debt.

In order to forgive my parents, I started with prayer. I had to ask God to give me the heart and desire to forgive them. My next step was to seek assistance from a Godly counselor, who would give me instructions on repairing the broken relationships. One of the critical assignments that assisted me with releasing the debt was writing a letter to my parents, communicating my feelings of anger and pain. I entitled one such letter "Why I Never Called You Daddy." Although, this was extremely difficult to share, I had to express the void and lack of emotional closeness in our relationship. These activities helped to liberate me from the bitterness I held towards my mother and father. However, the letters did not necessarily change the relationship immediately. In fact, it initially made the relationship worse. However, I had to accept the fact that they could never repay that debt, and in fact they were not even aware that they owed me anything. So in releasing the debt, I was freeing myself from the emotional bondage that held me captive.

A Heart to Forgive

What I describe as emotional debt is holding unforgiveness in your heart for actions that the debtor may or may not be aware of. They may have harmed you in some way, broken your heart, cheated on you, stolen from you and/or abused you; and you believe that they owe you something for harming you. At a minimum, you believe they owe you an apology and whatever you need them to do to right their wrong. Each time you interact with them or replay the memory in your mind, you add interest to the balance that you believe they owe you. But here is the challenge: you have to actually desire to release people of this emotional debt for your own sake. For me, God exposed this error in my heart. You see, I was holding a debt that I did not want to forgive.

As a Christian, it was hard to admit it, but this was how I felt toward my mother for so long. For years, I found it almost impossible to forgive her. Early on, my relationship with my mother had always been very close. As a single mother, she was my hero. When we left our country of Jamaica, I was nine years old, and life appeared to be promising. And it was initially. We lived with her fiancé, and this was the first time in my life that I'd ever lived with a male. My biological father lived in Canada with his family, so I did not know what it was like to live with a man. And this new experience was terrifying to me. Unfortunately, after a while, my mother's fiancé began to physically abuse my mother. This was absolutely horrifying to me because I did not know how to protect my mother from him. We were in a new country and far away from my family, and getting any kind of help seemed impossible. Although we wanted life to get better, the truth was that things continued to worsen. He sexually abused me. Although it took me a while to tell my mother, I eventually did. But we didn't have anywhere to go. At that point, my mother did move out of their room and stayed in mine; and we spent much time planning our escape. After my mother finally received approval for an apartment, we successfully moved out on a day while he was at work. This is such a powerful memory for me because we planned for months and eventually moved out on our own. For almost fifteen years, he did not know where we lived and how we were doing. At the time, I didn't really feel anything toward him because my mother and I never talked about it after we moved. But I finally felt safe.

However, in 2007, everything changed. One day when I arrived at her home, I saw that she had a beautiful bouquet of roses; I asked her who they were from. She informed me that they were from him. I was in so much shock, but I asked her what did that mean. Then she began to tell me that they were talking again and had planned to get married. I remember thinking, *This cannot be real. How could she marry him?* I asked her if she still believed what I said about him abusing me. She told me that it didn't happen that way. My heart shattered, because everything I thought about her changed. My mind went back to the day we moved out and I felt like she took it all back.

At that moment, I felt like she had betrayed me. She broke my heart. How could she love me and marry this man, after knowing what he did? I couldn't understand this. It was too painful to think about. It hurt too much. I felt as though I couldn't forgive her. In fact, I felt justified in my anger. And even if I was a Christian, this was not something I felt I could forgive.

I spent the next several years trying to ignore her, trying to ignore the pain. And for me, being busy was the only way I could function. I cut her out of my life. It was too painful to be around her. But after years of running and avoiding the issue, I knew it was time to ask the questions that had plagued my soul. God had put me in a corner and I knew that I needed to deal with this pain in my heart. It was time to forgive.

To begin the process, I attended a session on forgiveness taught by a Christian clinical psychologist, Dr. Grady. I knew that God was calling me to go through the pain in order to be free. But for so many years, I did not want to forgive my debtors because I did not think they deserved forgiveness. It would have been great if I had the desire to obey Christ when He told us to pray the prayer, "Forgive us our debts as we also have forgiven our debtors" (Matthew 6:12). But I did not want to forgive my mother. And I also wanted to punish her for betraying me. I thought if I forgave her, she would not receive the punishment I thought she deserved. But as I continued to study God's Word, He clarified why it was necessary to forgive. I needed to release this debt because that was what Jesus did for me. I began to see that my mother had her own struggles. It was also clear that I was harming myself by holding onto this anger and pain, and my future relationships would be impacted if I did not address it. I knew that one day, if God blessed me with children, these bitter roots would impact them as well, and I did not want to leave this legacy for them.

Over the course of a year, as I worked with my therapist to forgive my mother, things became clearer. As God promised, He blessed me because of my decision to forgive. This became apparent when I attended our church's Women's Day, entitled "Joy in the Journey." The speaker was a close friend and mentor to me. It was amazing to hear how God had masterfully woven together the seemingly broken strands of her life into something beautiful. One of the Scriptures she shared with us came from Exodus 23:20 (NLT): "See I am sending an angel before you to protect you on your journey and lead you safely to the place I have prepared for you."

This Scripture allowed me to reflect on my own journey and how God had placed angels all along my path. One angel in particular was a woman I met at a coffee shop while conducting a Bible study. After we began talking, she said she overheard me and wanted to talk to me. We spoke for hours and prayed together. Although this was a complete stranger, I knew from that moment that God put her in my life for a special reason. She prayed with me every day for months as I went through a season of depression. God placed her there to encourage me with her words, Scripture references, and prayer. She is still in my life and she is an absolute blessing.

The Cost of Un-forgiveness

> Then Peter came to Jesus and asked, 'Lord, how many times shall I forgive my brother or sister who sins against me? Up to seven times?' Jesus answered, 'I tell you, not seven times, but seventy-seven times. Therefore, the kingdom of heaven is like a king who wanted to settle accounts with his servants. As he began the settlement, a man who owed him ten thousand bags of gold was brought to him. Since he was not able to pay, the master ordered that he and his wife and his children and all that he had be sold to repay the debt. At this the servant fell on his knees before him. 'Be patient with me,' he begged, 'and I will pay back everything.' The servant's master took pity on him, canceled the debt and let him go. But when that servant went out, he found one of his fellow servants who owed him a hundred silver coins. He grabbed him and began to choke him. 'Pay back what you owe me!' he demanded. His fellow servant fell to his knees and begged him, 'Be patient with me, and I will pay it back.' But he refused. Instead, he went off and had the man thrown into prison until he could pay the debt. When the other servants saw what had happened, they were outraged and went and told their master everything that had happened. Then the master called the servant in. 'You wicked servant,' he said, 'I canceled all that debt of yours because you

begged me to. Shouldn't you have had mercy on your fellow servant just as I had on you?' In anger his master handed him over to the jailers to be tortured, until he should pay back all he owed. This is how my heavenly Father will treat each of you unless you forgive your brother or sister from your heart' (Matthew 18:21–35).

For years, I walked around with a large emotional debt in my heart. This debt that I carried around stole much of the joy that God planned for me. It stole years from me, years that I spent being angry and bitter. I lacked peace and joy because the debt was a burden that I felt in my heart. The largest challenge I had was that I did not want to give up the debt because I was angry with my mother. I wanted to hold onto it because I felt as though it was my obligation to make her feel the consequence for what she did. But I was the one who was actually paying the price. When you choose to hold onto anger and bitterness, you cannot restrict it to just one relationship. It tries to take over your heart, spilling over into other areas of your life.

The cost of un-forgiveness is developing unhealthy relationships. I believe this was the biggest burden I had. I couldn't understand why it was so hard to really trust others. Over time, I numbed my heart by focusing on my career goals, education, finances, and other relationships because I didn't want to feel the pain. However, God was calling me to search my heart and come to Him to find the things that I needed most.

Like the parable of the unmerciful servant, I was the one who chose to hold onto the offenses. It took me years to admit this. But it was true. I was unwilling to forgive my mother for years, but for so long I had forgotten how much I had been forgiven of, how much God had freed me from. Through years of individual therapy and joint sessions, I was able to release the debt that I believe she owed me. I had to study the Scriptures, pray, and cry it out to God for strength to release this. I made the decision at the beginning that I was going to go all the way through this.

As I continued to go to my therapy sessions, I had to come to grips with the fact that although my mother had made this choice, she was also a victim who had her own hurts and wounds. I remember crying out to God, asking Him why this happened to me; and in a still small voice, I heard Him say that I was no better. It was as though God was saying to me; your sins cost me the same thing, Jesus' life. Because of this, I have grown to forgive my mother as she has forgiven me of the things I've done to her. I learned that as Jesus has forgiven me and put me in right standing with the Father, I must also show mercy to others. But if I held onto the un-forgiveness, then it was no different than me sinning against God, and God cannot be associated with sin. The very thing God wants to free us from is the very thing that can keep us in bondage. When we do not forgive, we carry the sin of another person in our hearts. God said we must forgive our brother from our heart in order to not be treated like the wicked servant.

Emotional Release

> Come to me, all you who are weary and burdened, and I will give you rest. Take my yoke upon you and learn

Sabbath Season

from me, for I am gentle and humble in heart, and you will find rest for your souls. For my yoke is easy and my burden is light (Matthew 11:28–30).

According to an article in *Harvard Women's Health Watch*, "forgiving those who hurt you can improve your mental and physical well-being."[3] The article goes on to state that some of the benefits of forgiveness are reduced stress, better heart health, stronger relationships, reduced pain, and greater happiness. Research also shows that there are tremendous physical, emotional, and spiritual benefits that come from an individual's ability to forgive.

In order to experience the rest that comes from God, we must begin to recognize that we are burdened down by the weight of un-forgiveness. Once we acknowledge that we are held captive by our emotions, we can experience His rest by faith. God desires for us to be free from the emotional bondage that keeps us captive and prevents us from experiencing the joy and peace that He came to bring us. Jesus is able to look at us and see that we are helpless and harassed. He knows we are made of dust, and He can see straight to our emotional vulnerability. As you take time to enter your own Sabbath Season, you will begin to see that forgiveness has the power to release you spiritually of all the strongholds that keep you bound. God is calling us to a Sabbath delight; an opportunity for sweet fellowship with the Heavenly Father is awaiting us all. The Maker of

---

[3] Harvard Medical Publication. 2004. Power of Forgiveness-Forgive Others. http://www.health.harvard.edu/press_releases/power_of_forgiveness (Last accessed January 16, 2014).

Forgive Us Our Debts

the Universe desires to spend quality time with you so that you can be made whole. He wants time to tell you how He plans to lead and guide your life. And pray that this Scripture will rest in your heart:

> 'If you keep your feet from breaking the Sabbath and from doing as you please on my holy day, if you call the Sabbath a delight and the Lord's holy day honorable, and if you honor it by not going your own way and not doing as you please or speaking idle words, then you will find your joy in the Lord, and I will cause you to ride in triumph on the heights of the land and to feast on the inheritance of your father Jacob.' For the mouth of the Lord has spoken (Isaiah 58:13–14).

Sabbath Season

Sabbath Reflection

1. Are you currently struggling with un-forgiveness in your heart? If so, share below.

   _____
   _____
   _____
   _____
   _____
   _____
   _____
   _____
   _____
   _____
   _____
   _____
   _____

2. How are you holding on to an emotional or financial debt towards someone?

   _____
   _____
   _____
   _____
   _____

Forgive Us Our Debts

3. How has lack of forgiveness impacted your life?

Sabbath Season

4. Are you willing to pray about having a heart to release them from the debt they owe you? (Use the space below to write out your prayer.)

___
___
___
___
___
___
___
___
___
___
___
___
___
___

CHAPTER 4

Healing for Your Soul

"Then Jesus asked them, 'Which is lawful on the Sabbath: to do good or to do evil, to save life or to kill?' But they remained silent" (Mark 3:4).

The Sabbath is a great time to experience the healing power of Christ. As Jesus proclaimed to the people,

> The Spirit of the Sovereign Lord is on me, because the Lord has anointed me to proclaim good news to the poor. He has sent me to bind up the brokenhearted, to proclaim freedom for the captives and release from darkness for the prisoners, to proclaim the year of the Lord's favor and the day of vengeance of our God, to comfort all who mourn, and provide for those who grieve in Zion—to bestow on them a crown of beauty instead of ashes, the oil of joy instead of mourning, and a garment of praise instead of a spirit of despair. They will be called oaks of righteousness, a planting of the Lord for the display of his splendor (Isaiah 61:1–3).

Sabbath Season

As the Son of God, He proved to the people that not only did He come to fulfill the law, but to also bring forth healing and restoration to the lost and dying. He often performed many miracles, even on the Sabbath, and these actions seemed to challenge the traditions created by the religious leaders of His day. As we have already learned from the Scriptures, literally refusing to rest from doing any kind of work on the Sabbath was viewed as a violation of the law. But as Jesus revealed to the people, the Sabbath was made for man and should never take precedent over fulfilling the work of God. In turn, Jesus challenged the religious constructs that the Israelites dogmatically held to regarding Sabbath principles. He forced them to consider that even if someone was hurting and wounded on the Sabbath, He must help those in need, regardless of what day it was. As such, I learned from my Sabbath Season that this time was not only to rest the body and soul, but to receive the healing that came from the Lord.

Sabbath Healing

Let us examine an example of healing on the Sabbath:

Some time later, Jesus went up to Jerusalem for one of the Jewish festivals. Now there is in Jerusalem near the Sheep Gate a pool, which in Aramaic is called Bethesda and which is surrounded by five covered colonnades. Here a great number of disabled people used to lie—the blind, the lame, the paralyzed. One who was there had been an invalid for thirty-eight years. When Jesus saw him lying there and learned that he had been in this condition for a long time, he asked him, 'Do you want to get well?' 'Sir,' the invalid replied, 'I have no one to help me into the pool when the water is stirred. While I am trying to get in, someone else goes down ahead of me.' Then Jesus said to him, 'Get up! Pick up your mat and walk.' At once the man was cured; he picked up his mat and walked. The day on which this took place was a Sabbath, and so the Jewish leaders said to the man who had been healed, 'It is the Sabbath; the law forbids you to carry your mat.' But he replied, 'The man who made me well said to me, 'Pick up your mat and walk.' So they asked him, 'Who is this fellow who told you to pick it up and walk?' The man who was healed had no idea who it was, for Jesus had slipped away into the crowd that was there. Later Jesus found him at the temple and said to him, 'See, you are well again. Stop sinning or something worse may happen to you.' The man went away and told the Jewish leaders that it was Jesus who had made him well. So, because Jesus was doing these things on the Sabbath, the Jewish leaders began to persecute him. In his defense Jesus said to them, 'My Father is always at his work to this very day, and I too am working' (John 5:1–17).

In a way, we can view this passage as a type of counseling session for this paralyzed man, who had been an invalid for thirty-eight years. God demonstrated His desire to not just heal this man physically, but He offered him emotional and spiritual healing as well, ultimately freeing him from the bondage that held him in captivity for decades. Jesus addressed the emotional and spiritual paralysis, which was far more significant than his physical illness.

Sabbath Season

In this passage, I want to focus on the question Jesus asked the paralyzed man: "Do you want to get well?" What a question to ask someone who's been paralyzed for thirty-eight years! Most of us would never dare ask that question, because we just assume that the answer to the question would be a resounding, "yes!" But Jesus saw something in that man, which made Him ask that question. Jesus wanted the man to confront the condition that quickly became his identity. What did He see? Was something holding this man back? Was he hiding in his illness? Had he grown accustomed to being paralyzed? There are so many questions rooted in that question Jesus asked.

Like this paralyzed man, I was saying I wanted to get well from all my emotional wounds I had. But I was unwilling to get the help that I needed to heal. I was unwilling to be still long enough to hear what God really wanted me to do. For years, God was asking me this question, "Do you want to get well?" He was asking me to deal with the emotional pain and hurt of the past. But my answer for years was, "no." I did not want to acknowledge that something might be wrong with my life. I wanted to pretend that I was not hurting; rather, I created a façade and convinced myself and others that I was okay. But underneath it all, I knew something was wrong.

Whenever we go through our hardships that leave us wounded, we have to answer "yes" to God's question of whether or not we want to be well. And in order to answer affirmatively, we have to admit that something is wrong. For me, saying "yes" meant:

Healing for Your Soul

1. I didn't have it all together.
2. I was broken.
3. I needed help.
4. I really didn't have control.
5. I had to be vulnerable.
6. I might appear weak to others.
7. I wasn't well.

Healing begins with admitting that you need help. You must decide that you want to be healed. The Scripture is very clear in that God has given us a choice on whether or not we really want to confront our illness. This is because many of us have grown accustomed and maybe even comfortable with our condition. Jesus said, "It is not the healthy who need a doctor, but the sick" (Luke 5:31). In denying our need for healing, we deny Jesus' access to our hearts. Jesus recognized that a major condition of our heart was pride. If we are unable to admit to ourselves that we are broken vessels, then He has no pathway into our lives in order to perform the miraculous healing.

When Jesus asked the paralyzed man if he wanted to get well, he responded by saying, "I have no one to help me into the pool when the water is stirred. While I am trying to get in, someone else goes down ahead of me." This man had been lying there for almost forty years and he could not get his healing. He had been waiting for someone to come by and help him. And in a way, we are just like him. Are you waiting for someone to help you? Well, Jesus is saying get up. He is asking us to go after our healing. For many of us, we have access to healing, but are we going after it? For years, I knew that I needed help, and I made many half-hearted attempts to address the issue. But I was not aggressive about getting help. In my heart of hearts, I was truly blind to the severity of my own condition.

This man was sitting in the same position for almost forty years. God wants us to recognize that no one can get in our way when we have faith to believe that we can receive our healing. You hold the key to beginning the journey to your own healing. Sounding familiar? It begins with your faith. Research has shown that the Christian faith is an important factor in areas of overcoming and coping with physical illness. We need to talk about the power of faith in healing people from all kinds of illnesses. Our faith makes a difference in our healing.

Are you crying out for help? Could anyone or anything get in your way if you realized that you needed help? Or if you saw that your ability to get well was just a few feet away. God was doing a heart check with this man at the pool in Bethesda, exposing that he was not fully invested in his own healing. Are you willing to get your healing no matter the cost? My modern day Sabbath Season included the important decision to heal. This decision was incredibly challenging as I began to embark on a journey to heal the issues that plagued me since my childhood. I recognized that therapy was going to be an imperative part of the journey. I knew that this would require all my time, energy, and focus; and I could no longer run. Jesus was offering me healing during my Sabbath time, and God could be calling you to take time to address deep wounds during your Sabbath Season. For some of you, therapy may not be the answer for whatever the reason; but the Godly counsel I received was instrumental in my healing process.

As Jesus demonstrated back then, He has the authority to heal on the Sabbath; and if you are willing, He will perform a miracle in your life. Allow Jesus to heal you during your Sabbath. Allow yourself to be still long enough to admit that you are not well. Our Sabbath experience is a time that opens the door to God's healing power. You must choose to be healed by answering the question: Do you want to get well? Has Jesus asked you that question, and if so, what is your answer?

Healing is in Your Obedience

God could have simply told the man that he was healed, and it would have been done for him as He commanded. However, He told him to get up and pick up his mat, which violated the religious leaders' traditions. If this man did not obey God, he would not have been healed. Like the paralytic, God is calling us to put our faith into action. This man could have easily questioned the seemingly impossible command to "pick up [his] mat;" and if he spent time trying to use logic to figure out how he was going to do it, he would have missed his blessing. His healing came as a result of his act of obedience to God's word. We all may have requested something from God that appeared impossible. But in order to get our blessing, we have to obey the Word of God in our lives.

At some point in our lives, we will all experience some kind of wound, whether it is emotional, spiritual, or

Sabbath Season

physical. To find help for our physical wounds and ailments, many of us go to the doctor. I remember when my best friend had brain surgery. For years, she didn't know what caused her stroke as a teenager. However, while she was pregnant with her first child, they learned that she had a large brain tumor. The doctors decided to wait until after she had her beautiful daughter to perform the procedure. Right before she went in for surgery, I asked her if she wanted to pray, and she said yes. After we opened our eyes, her neurosurgeon had joined our circle of prayer. This was a powerful moment, because although he was the head of the neurology department at the hospital and one of only a few doctors who performed that procedure, he still relied on God. God is our true physician and we can find healing for our alignments through the talented physicians He created. However, people can often times be insensitive to their physical needs by not allowing proper time to heal because they may, for example, need to be back at work. This happens partly because of pressure from the work culture, but also internal pressures that come from not knowing how to rest. But how do we treat the less visible emotional wounds, the ones that we may not see with our human eyes, the wounds that affect our hearts and our spirit?

Many of us have deep wounds from our childhood and our past. We also have spiritual wounds where we've been hurt by church family; we may even believe that God has wounded us because something happened that we could not explain. Too often, we carry these wounds around, and instead of addressing them, we just avoid the person who offended us. And because of that, many of us become angry with God. But the Word clearly states that if we have anything against our brother, we are to confront it before we bring our sacrifice to Him. It matters to God whether or not we have spiritual wounds. He wants us to bring our pain and frustrations to Him, and we have many examples to follow from the Bible. David prayed about everything. He prayed about the good, the bad, and the ugly things in life. He brought it all before God. Paul prayed about a thorn in his flesh, pleading with God to remove it. He eventually got to a place where he just had to accept that this was something he was going to have to live with. The main lesson I learned from all of this was that they brought all their troubles to God. They laid their fears, frustrations, and hurts before the Father.

As I mentioned earlier, I carried around deep wounds that I buried in my heart. As a child, I would internalize my struggles, believing that it was my fault that these things were happening to me. I did not know how to process it. I didn't know if I should go to my family or not, because we didn't really talk about stuff like this. I chose not to speak about my feelings of sadness and loneliness for a long time. But I learned that Jesus wanted to heal me as He desires to heal you from all your troubles; He wants to make us whole. And as I discovered, the Sabbath Season was a time where I could find healing for my soul, and so can you.

Many of us are in search of a peace, the peace that surpasses all understanding, as described in Philippians. Jesus wants to give us this healing and it can be found in no

Sabbath Season

one else. The Sabbath is meant to be a time of liberation, forgiveness, and healing from the things that hold us captive. And if you will obey the voice of the Lord, you will find that your Sabbath rest is the place where you can be free and whole to worship God from a healed and pure heart.

Healing for Your Soul

Sabbath Reflection

1. Do you feel like the man at the pool in Bethesda? If so, in what way(s)?

   _____
   _____
   _____
   _____
   _____
   _____
   _____
   _____
   _____
   _____
   _____
   _____
   _____

2. What way do you feel emotionally, physically or spiritually stuck?

   _____
   _____
   _____
   _____
   _____
   _____
   _____

Sabbath Season

3. What are some things that get in the way when you attempt to change?

4. Do you believe that God can heal you? (Describe)

Healing for Your Soul

CHAPTER FIVE

Sabbath Delight

'If you keep your feet from breaking the Sabbath and from doing as you please on my holy day, if you call the Sabbath a delight and the Lord's holy day honorable, and if you honor it by not going your own way and not doing as you please or speaking idle words, then you will find your joy in the Lord, and I will cause you to ride in triumph on the heights of the land and to feast on the inheritance of your father Jacob.' For the mouth of the Lord has spoken (Isaiah 58:13–14).

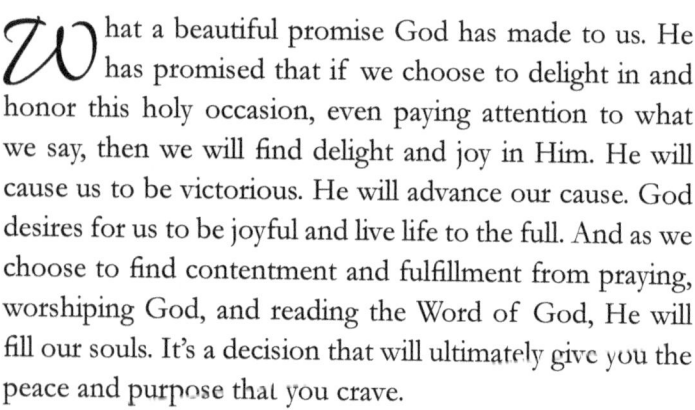

What a beautiful promise God has made to us. He has promised that if we choose to delight in and honor this holy occasion, even paying attention to what we say, then we will find delight and joy in Him. He will cause us to be victorious. He will advance our cause. God desires for us to be joyful and live life to the full. And as we choose to find contentment and fulfillment from praying, worshiping God, and reading the Word of God, He will fill our souls. It's a decision that will ultimately give you the peace and purpose that you crave.

This is an incredible honor to seek out and find purpose in His word. God wants us to choose Him. For a long time, I would read the Word and pray, but not with a sense of

Sabbath Delight

excitement and joy. My relationship with God had become lackluster and I struggled to have the desire to read His Word and pray. I also didn't know what my purpose was, and that made it difficult for me in my walk. I knew there was something more that I should be doing, but I didn't know how to get there. Although I knew reading the Word and praying was the right thing to do, I just found it difficult to choose this. Furthermore, I would often get distracted and lose focus on the Word. The worries of life would often steal my faith and convictions. I felt that I was just running from one thing to the next, jumping from activities, to work, to church, to various relationships; and many times, I wouldn't have a strong sense of purpose to guide my activities. So, after years of trying to will myself into doing these things and failing, I decided to begin to search my heart and pray specifically for the desire to continue to do what was right so that I would delight myself in the Lord.

There was a joy and passion missing from my life. It seemed like a simple thing, but I just wasn't happy, even after I attained all the things I thought I wanted. The reason was that I hadn't addressed the internal things that I needed to address. The material possessions were not going to make up for the hole in my heart. I didn't know exactly what caused it, but I knew that it was something that I needed to bring to God. And during my Sabbath Season, I learned that delighting myself in the Lord would bring me the comfort, peace, and happiness that I was after. It was a time where I ran to God emotionally, I laughed at the funny things He did in my life and I made it priority in my day to identify the special things God did just for me throughout my day.

Sabbath Season

Made Just for You

"The Sabbath was made for man, not man for the Sabbath" (Mark 2:27). The beauty of this day is that God made it just for you. It's a blessed experience that God designed to allow us to rest, relax, and rejuvenate. It is a holy and special time. God is amazing in that He designed and tailor-made a time that was just for us. He considered what we would need for generations: a time to connect and restore. There is nothing you can do to earn it; however, it's available for those who have the faith to enter into it.

I remember wondering if I would get bored taking this Sabbath journey with God. But as I became still and learned who God was, He began to fill my mind with so many ideas and visions for my life. This book is a product of that time as God gave me the vision for it while on my journey. Although I resisted this for a long time, I now understand that this was a platform to encourage others as they take their own Sabbath journey.

We are all seeking happiness and purpose, but we find it when we call on God. I would often invest my time in things that I believed would make me happy, only to later find out that this type of joy and happiness was temporary. God makes a promise to give us a steady stream of joy when we honor the Sabbath. He knows exactly what brings you joy and He will give you those things if you delight in Him. As the Scriptures read, "Take delight in the LORD, and he will give you the desires of your heart" (Psalm 37:4).

Sabbath Delight

Connecting with God

One of the single most beneficial elements of observing a time of Sabbath is our ability to connect with God. As the Bible states, "The Lord is near to all who call on him, to all who call on him in truth" (Psalm 145:18). There is no limit on how close we can draw to God. God has left it up to us to determine how close we are to Him. We must make the time to carve out the moments, minutes, hours, days, and seasons that we are going to commit our time, energy, and focus to God. There are so many things fighting for our attention, and the more connected we become with other things, the more difficult it is to disconnect and unplug from the world. These distractions are different for each person. For me, I remember how I wasted so much time on the Internet and social media. Sometimes I would look up one thing and then an hour later, I forgot what I started looking at in the first place, and end up on some random blog or newsfeed. This was another thing that stole my time from the Lord. The Sabbath is literally a time where you stop working. You power down your phone, laptop, and other electronic devices, not because you are trying to be legalistic, but to demonstrate to God that you want to give Him your undivided attention. And in order to connect with God, we have to first decide that this is what we want to do. Next, we need to pray for the heart to do this. The more we take time to find joy in God, the more He takes time to find joy in us. He wants to bless us. God is longing for us to choose Him.

Sabbath Season

To further illustrate the importance of connecting with the Father during the Sabbath, I want to ask you the following question: Have you ever eaten a meal with someone who continued to check his or her phone while you were talking to them? How did that make you feel? Whenever that happened to me, I felt insulted; it was rude and insensitive. Ironically, I found myself doing the same thing to another, and I'm sure the person speaking to me saw it as being rude. In a way, this can make a person feel like you do not value their time. Now, think about how God feels when we are constantly choosing things over spending time with Him. When we repeatedly neglect a time of Sabbath, we neglect what really matters most, and that is spending time with the Father, and developing our relationship with Him. If we do not spend time nurturing and cultivating our relationship, we will soon have a dry walk.

As you read the Word and begin to pray, the Holy Spirit will prompt you with things to do. I recall certain moments during my Sabbath Season when I would sneak away to my favorite prayer spot and pour out my heart to God. I remember the Lord calling me, saying "Come and talk to me." And when I did, I was able to release all the burdens that I had unknowingly picked up over the years. During this "down time," I learned to hear the voice of the Spirit more clearly; and at times, He would instruct me to share my faith with other people. For example, I remember when the Lord told me to go and speak to a young woman that I met at a coffee shop. I remember thinking, *I am not sure if she would be open to hearing the message, but I'm going to share with her anyway.* At that time, I wasn't working and I was in the middle of my Sabbath Season. As I tried to explain this to her, all I kept thinking was, *This probably sounds crazy.* But I was obedient and shared my life with her anyway. We eventually exchanged contact information and went on our way. I kept her phone number, but didn't call her. (I know.) But a few months later, she called me to ask where my church was. From that point on, she came to church every Sunday, and we began studying the Bible together. She was later baptized and became a disciple of Christ. This is one of those experiences where I learned to be obedient to the Holy Spirit and allowed Him to guide me. And the Sabbath Season that you take will cause you to hear the Lord as well; you must be adamant in obeying the instructions He has for you.

Connecting with Others

Observing the Sabbath is also about spending quality time with our family and fellow believers. One of our greatest gifts on earth is our physical and spiritual family. However, with our busy schedules, we can fail to connect with our loved ones. As I mentioned in previous chapters, in the Jewish culture, the Sabbath was not only a specific time in which no work was done, but it was also an opportunity for families to connect. During my Sabbath Season, I had a chance to visit my family and spend extended time uniting with them. I also had time to pray and share my faith.

In our busy-body, American culture, we are often running around with multiple activities. I have counseled families whose schedules are so busy that they rarely see or spend time with each other during the weekdays. And their weekends are just as busy; they try to incorporate so many activities for their children that they are just running from one sports event to another dance recital. This is unfortunate because the opportunity to really connect with one another is missed. Often times, families no longer share meals together or create times for family devotion. But when we set a specific time to observe what God has designed for us, we help build and maintain the bonds of family, which is so important in today's time. We need to prioritize time to connect with our families.

Connecting to Your Purpose

One of the greatest moments in life is when you discover what you were created for. God has an incredible purpose and calling on each of our lives. At times, we can waste time looking toward the wrong thing to find our purpose. However, the more we look to God, the more we will find our purpose and calling in Him.

To know your purpose is to know why you are here, why you were born into your family, and why you experienced the things that you did. For so long I was searching for my purpose. I would look to different jobs and career goals to find my purpose. But I learned that attaining the title and the goals I set out for myself did not satisfy the internal longing I had for something greater. We know that we are here to do God's will, which is to love Him and love others.

Sabbath Delight

But what exactly was I here to do? Why did God make me? Finding out the answer to these questions radically changed my life. When I realized that God wanted me to teach others about entering into His rest, He gave me a dream in my heart that I knew only He could fulfill.

As you devote quality time to the Lord, you will witness His ability to share with you what He intends for you to do with your life. You will no longer waste time on things that are not aligned with your purpose. Your mission will become clearer and your time on earth will be more valuable because you know that God has a mission for you to complete.

Enjoy Your Life

"There is nothing better for a person than that he should eat and drink and find enjoyment in his toil. This also, I saw, is from the hand of God" (Ecclesiastes 2:24, ESV). God created this Sabbath time in order for us to enjoy life. If we are not careful, we can become bored and miserable, and lose sight of the joy of life. Joy is not determined by our circumstance, but rather from the many blessings that come from God. It is He who gives us joy. The Sabbath is a time to re-discover the child-like joy that comes from life. God wants us to laugh again, for as He says in Proverbs 17:22, "a cheerful heart is good medicine."

As you look to embark on your Sabbath Season, remember to play and run. Remember the things that make you happy. Paint, sing, dance, draw, write, laugh, skip, hop,

Sabbath Season

swim, dream, and remember the joys of life. Become a person who makes others around you happy. Help others remember to find the joy of life.

Sabbath Delight

Sabbath Reflection

1. Habakkuk 2:2 encourages us to write the vision and make a plan. Has God placed a dream or vision on your heart? If so, use the space below to write out the vision.

   _____
   _____
   _____
   _____
   _____
   _____
   _____
   _____
   _____
   _____
   _____
   _____
   _____

2. What is holding you back from your dream? List out any fears and/or doubts you may have about pursuing this dream.

   _____
   _____

Sabbath Season

3. If you're unsure about your dream or vision, are you willing to pray and seek out God's Word in order to find your purpose? (Write out your prayer)

Sabbath Delight

4. What are some activities that you enjoyed doing, but haven't done in a while? Take a moment to remember the things that brought you joy. (Example: Drawing, Painting, Singing, Sewing, etc.)

CHAPTER SIX

God's Supernatural Provision

Follow my decrees and be careful to obey my laws, and you will live safely in the land. Then the land will yield its fruit, and you will eat your fill and live there in safety. You may ask, 'What will we eat in the seventh year if we do not plant or harvest our crops?' I will send you such a blessing in the sixth year that the land will yield enough for three years. While you plant during the eighth year, you will eat from the old crop and will continue to eat from it until the harvest of the ninth year comes in (Leviticus 25: 18–22).

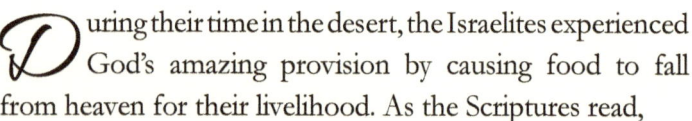

During their time in the desert, the Israelites experienced God's amazing provision by causing food to fall from heaven for their livelihood. As the Scriptures read,

> Each morning everyone gathered as much as they needed, and when the sun grew hot, it melted away. On the sixth day, they gathered twice as much—two omers for each person—and the leaders of the community came and reported this to Moses. He said to them, 'This is what the Lord commanded: 'Tomorrow is to be a day of Sabbath rest, a holy Sabbath to the Lord. So bake

God's Supernatural Provision

what you want to bake and boil what you want to boil. Save whatever is left and keep it until morning' (Exodus 16:21–23).

God made sure that they had what they needed, and even provided double for them so they could remember to observe the Sabbath. God expected His people to continue honoring the Lord's Day. Although their lack of faith contributed to their wilderness experience, they continued to witness the supernatural provision of God.

The Israelites had this miracle take place for forty years while they were in the wilderness. God took care of them and made sure that their needs were met. He made sure that their clothes never wore out. And like the children of Israel, I learned that God would be my provider if I continued to honor my time with Him.

Over the course of my Sabbath Season, I witnessed God's provisions that I could only say was nothing but the hand of God. He opened doors for me to walk through. He also closed doors in order for me to see that He wanted to provide so much more for me. God had something specific and uniquely designed for me. Let me give you some examples. First, God provided me with a Christian counselor to guide me through some of the most difficult times. As I have already alluded to in prior chapters, this counselor knew exactly what I needed to be healed from my wounds. God not only placed this counselor before me, but He also positioned other Christians in my life to encourage me and to take care of me on my journey. He made sure that I had what I needed.

Sabbath Season

In addition to that, God gave me resources that I knew were from Him. When God placed it on my heart to write this book, I had no tools, like a computer, to get it done. God placed it on the heart of a dear friend to invest in this venture by giving me her own laptop. She expressed that she wanted to support and bless me, and I am so grateful to have friends like her. But He did not stop there. God also used my father, who gave me enough money to cover two months living expenses during my Sabbath Season. He was unaware of this decision that I made to enter into this rest; however, I knew that God was demonstrating his supernatural provisions. This was the first time in my life that my father had sent me that much money at one time.

During my Sabbath Season, I lived in my apartment for nine months and was able to live off of my savings that God provided during the year. I never went without. He met every single one of my needs. During my time, I was able to travel and to spend time with friends and families. I quickly learned that the Sabbath trains us to depend and rely of God. When we observe it, we consistently cultivate a dependence on God for all our needs. We become keenly aware of His power and ability to provide all that we need. And this leads to supernatural peace. When we are with God, we can rest from the storms of life because He is the only one that says to the storms, "Quiet! Be still!" (Mark 4:39).

I realize that for some people, the idea of taking a season to devote entirely to God could seem frightening. But God is more than able to take care of you. During this time, He allowed me to earn my clinical license, which allowed me to practice independently. This offered me flexibility to complete this book and to work on the other things that God had placed on my heart. God continued to demonstrate to me that He would meet all of my needs, and He would do the same for you.

I must be frank and say that this was not easy for me. I struggled to embrace this period because I was used to doing things myself. I was uncomfortable having limits on spending money because money had always been a source of security and stability for me. I always felt comfortable when I had a large amount saved up. However, during this time, God taught me that He was the source of my security; that He was the one that ultimately controlled my bank account. I learned to put my trust in God and not what I could financially accomplish for myself. So much of my confidence and self-esteem came from my own ability to provide and to make things happen. But during the Sabbath, God will tell us to put those things and that ability down.

At the end of the year, I knew that God wanted me to move forward. My life was changing. Furthermore, people were also noticing that I was changing. God was removing the feelings of depression that lingered in my heart. God was changing my life and moving me toward my purpose. Not only had He provided the finances for me, but He also provided the kind of comfort and healing that I longed for regarding my mother. During this time, she encouraged me and supported me. I began to see how much she truly cared about me. Although our relationship was not always the greatest, she was consistent in her support and assistance over this season. This book would not have been possible without my mother's support. She supported my journey to share this story and has financially supported my venture. This is proof about what God can do, if you trust Him. His provisions are truly heaven-sent. There's no other way I can explain it.

Multiply His Glory

Do the math. The Sabbath Season is a time where you contribute nothing and God contributes everything. We remember that anything times zero equals zero. So how is it possible to gain while in season of rest? Well, this is the formula that God has come up with to produce the most glory. See, in this equation, He gets all the glory. God wants to demonstrate His glory to the world and this can be done by us resting in the fact that we know He will meet our needs. When we rest from our work, God will multiply our faith in order to demonstrate His glory.

Expect a Harvest

During my Sabbath Season, God worked on my faith. He showed me that it is possible to expect something from Him without my human effort. This is a level of faith that I did not understand. God promised to bless my life without any of my works. But don't get me wrong, observing a Sabbath Season is challenging. It will test your faith to totally trust in God. It also removes the false idea that you have the power and control to create things. God is the only one that can create something from nothing, and He has proven that He is able to make something appear from the abyss of life.

God's Supernatural Provision

When I speak with others about the idea of taking time to rest, I remind them that the Sabbath Season is an opportunity to observe God's miraculous and creative force at work in their lives. Just as God created the world with everything that it needs to survive, God created you with everything you need in Christ. You will see God create resources, opportunities, relationships, and finances from literally nothing. He made man from dust, so is anything impossible for Him? He is not bound to the limitations of our mind and therefore can arrange circumstances and resources that we would never dream of. According to Isaiah 55:8, His thoughts and ways are far beyond us.

The Sabbath rest is for us. The principles of the Sabbath are still critical and necessary elements in our walk with God. The Sabbath teaches us to have faith and to be obedient when He calls us to Him. Our relationship with God is not about our works, but about God being at work in us. The Sabbath is a reminder that God does not need our human efforts to create things. He only needs our faith.

God has called each one of us to enter His rest, to live off the bounty of His land and be obedient to His plan for our lives. However, we will never enter this rest if we lack faith and are disobedient to God. As it is stated in Hebrews, "we ought to tremble with fear that some of you might fail to experience it [His rest]" (Hebrews 4:1, NLT). God has something amazing for each one of us. However, our ability to experience this place of rest depends on our ability to have faith. God expects us to believe and trust in Him in order to enter this place He has created just for you.

Sabbath Season

Sabbath Reflection

1. Have you experienced God's supernatural provisions in your life? If so, in what way(s)?

   _____
   _____
   _____
   _____
   _____
   _____
   _____
   _____
   _____
   _____
   _____
   _____
   _____

2. Are you struggling to trust that God will provide for you in any area of your life? If so, describe below.

   _____
   _____
   _____
   _____

God's Supernatural Provision

3. What memories and Scripture(s) encourage you when you doubt that God will provide for you?

Sabbath Season

4. Do you trust God to meet all of your needs? If so, are you willing to take a Sabbath, even if it might mean making financial adjustments? Share below.

_____
_____
_____
_____
_____
_____
_____
_____
_____
_____
_____
_____
_____
_____

CHAPTER SEVEN

Lessons from My Sabbath Season

"The Lord is my shepherd, I lack nothing. He makes me lie down in green pastures, he leads me beside quiet waters, he refreshes my soul" (Psalm 23:1–3a).

"For everything, there is a season, and a time for every matter under heaven" (Ecclesiastes 3:1, ESV).

The Sabbath Season is truly a special and unique time with God; He has designed it for all of humanity. He blessed it and made it a holy and sacred time. It's an honor and privilege to have this intimate period with the Maker of the Universe. He calls us into this place, a shelter from the worries of the world. He teaches us to cultivate a dependency on Him like a father would with a child. One of the beauties of the Sabbath is that we discover God is our inheritance. He alone supplies all our needs. When we are filled with Him, we have everything we need. If we are children of God then we are also considered heirs (Romans 8:17).

To conclude this book, I want to leave the reader with several small lessons that I developed during my period of rest with the Lord. I learned to:

Sabbath Season

- *Hear the Voice of God*—When we enter this kind of Sabbath, we learn how to hear and respond to the voice of God. As Jesus said, "My sheep listen to my voice; I know them, and they follow me" (John 10:27). However when we're constantly running around, we can disconnect from God. During my Sabbath, I had nothing but time to deal with the things I was running from. As I learned, God will open up the wounds that we've covered up for years and allow His word and His Spirit to heal us. He will walk with us through the valley of the shadow of death. My Sabbath Season witnessed more crying, more praying, more singing, and more petitioning of the Father than any other time in my life. And when we are in this place, we cannot avoid the things that are troubling our minds. As I continued to pour out my heart to the Lord, He began to speak to me concerning my life and the direction in which He was leading me.

- *Trust God as the Source of Everything*—Some times when we are self-reliant and independent, we can get our roles confused. We think we are making things happen. Although this might be true on some levels, the truth is that it happens only because God allows it to happen. I learned to trust God for everything. I became aware and more conscious of the fact that God is the source of all things. The things that I accomplished or will accomplish are only because of God. My source is not my job, my friends, my relationship, or my bank account. No, these are the things God has allowed me to have, and I had to remember that He was the source of it all.

- *Let go and Let God, Truly*—Our nation is known for its independent culture. We are known for pulling ourselves up by our boot straps. We prefer being in control. However, during the Sabbath, we are to put down our independence and depend on God. We learn to let go of control. And a funny thing happens: life goes on without us. It's a great reminder that we don't hold the world up. Ministries will function; jobs will continue after you take time off. We put a lot of pressure on ourselves to perform and hold things together. However, we should always remember that it's God who controls everything and sometimes He may ask us to loosen our grip on an area in our lives in order to teach us to depend on Him.

- *Trust in God's Provision*—God has always provided for me, emotionally, physically, spiritually, and financially. He placed people in my life that understood my journey and supported my decision. During my Sabbath Season, I understood life more clearly than at any other time. He removed relationships and put new ones in that encouraged me on my way.

Sabbath Season

- *Trust His Timing*—He showed me that His timing was perfect. When we plant anything in the ground, it is God who makes it grow. In like manner, He knows what we need to grow into the man or woman of God we need to be. For example, during that year, I realized that I was eligible to sit for my board exam, and I was able to study and pass it. God created this opportunity for me to study and prepare for my test. In entering into this year, God allowed me to save, pay off my car, and be put in a position to live off my savings. At no other time would I have been prepared for this. I was also in a place where I wanted to be prepared for my future, and so I was open to doing the work necessary to heal, even though I had no idea what that meant at the time. I can tell you so many things about God's perfect timing and how He intervened in my life at just the right time. I praise God that everything worked for my good.

- *Put Faith in God to Create New Things*—We learn that God can create things out of nothing. There was no substance when He created this world. So it's not too difficult for Him to give us ideas and create new opportunities in places and ways we've never dreamed of. His word is the foundation by which we can build and create things with the seed that He plants in our hearts. The promises come by faith (Romans 4:16).

Lessons from My Sabboth Season

- *Relinquish My Hurts to Him*—During this time, I learned to go to the Father for all my answers. Although others may give good advice, it's important to go to God first. He has all the answers to the questions we have. We often go to our friends and companions before praying and consulting God. However, God wants to be our first love; He wants us to run to Him first. He says to come to Him when we are weary and tired.

- *Restore my Relationship with the Father*—God wants us to take time to repair, restore, and rejuvenate our relationship with Him. We learn to put the Father in His rightful place. It's easy to grow distant from God, missing a quiet time here and there. We end up lacking focus in our Bible study. And the worries of the world can take over our thoughts and overwhelm us. But God wants an intimate relationship with us, even when we go through difficult times.

- *Enjoy Life Again*—Busyness can oftentimes cause us to miss the simple joys of life. There are beautiful things happening every day. However, when we're rushing to the next event and checking off the to-do list too often, we miss the pleasures of life. God wants us to enjoy His creation. Yes, we are to work the land, but we are also to enjoy what He's created for us.

- *Surrender Everything to God*—Surrendering is a hard one. It's knowing that you have a plan and a way that you want things done, but deciding to give up control and giving it to God. It also entails surrendering your fears and deciding that not following God is worse than your fear. By entering this season, I had to give up my plans. I wanted my certain relationships, but I had to surrender and trust God. I wanted to continue my job, but I had to trust God and allow Him to heal me in His way. I wanted to get another job immediately because it was uncomfortable and unfamiliar just being still. But I learned how to trust God for everything, especially when I felt anxious.

- *See that God is my Inheritance*—One of the best lessons I've learned is that God, the Maker of the Universe, is my inheritance. As the Psalmist says, "Lord, you alone are my inheritance, my cup of blessing. You guard all that is mine. The land you have given me is a pleasant land. What a wonderful inheritance! I will bless the Lord who guides me; even at night my heart instructs me. I know the Lord is always with me. I will not be shaken, for he is right beside me. No wonder my heart is glad, and I rejoice. My body rests in safety" (Psalm 16: 5-9, NLT). In our hectic schedule, we might be wondering, how can we find time to rest? The answer to that question really begins with opening your heart and mind. We all make time for the things that we need to do.

If someone told me I could earn a million dollars if I set aside a few hours each week, then, let's just say, I would be on it! Everyone in my life would be on notice that I have to devote this time, and I'm sure that they would understand. In fact, they would probably want to know how they could get in on this deal. Well, you know where I'm going with this. Our reward for setting aside time isn't one million dollars. It's actually better than a million because we have time with the One who created the power to get wealth and is the source of everything. God is our inheritance. He contains all the blessings we will ever need, although we can lose focus and believe that our relationship, our jobs, bank accounts, and other things are the source. When we enter into His rest, we remember that God alone has everything that we need.

- *Create Again*—When they want inspiration to create something new, many artists go away to write or paint. This was something I did during my Sabbath. In reducing the amount of time I contributed to other things like television and radio, I opened the door for God to invest and create new visions in my heart. During that time, I created a group for women called "Wonderfully Made." I also started a book club. Many other ventures have come to me, and had I not chosen to take this path, they would never come to fruition. God has given me numerous ideas and dreams and I'm excited to see what God will do.

- *Grow my Harvest with my Faith*—During this time of rest, the critical element that you must have is faith. Your faith in God will drive you to the promised land. Your ability to believe in the promise of God will be the necessary component to help your harvest grow. It is our faith that releases God to reward us with the blessing that He prepared for us long ago. See, God does not need us to work to create these blessings. It's already done! He created them for us when He created the world. All He needs is our faith to join along with Him. Our faith activates the blessings and brings them into full manifestation in the physical realm. However, if we doubt and complain, we will not see the promises of God unfold in our lives. The Israelites are our greatest example of missing out on the promise of God because of their lack of faith. However, today many of us are missing out on the incredible rest that God has planned for us because of our lack of faith. But we must determine to do as God desires.

While this journey may have presented its own challenges, I am very grateful that the Lord took me on it. Not only did He heal me of all my wounds, but He restored broken relationships that would have otherwise remained dysfunctional. Nothing in the world could have

Lessons from My Sabboth Season

prepared me for this time period, and nothing in the world compares to the immeasurable wisdom and knowledge I gained as a result of taking this Sabbath Season with the Lord. I pray that my testimony encourages you to venture down this road as well, and watch how God comes through for you.

Sabbath Season

Sabbath Reflection

1. Do you believe God is your greatest inheritance?

2. Are you ready to enter your own Sabbath Season?

Lessons from My Sabboth Season

3. How has God called you to enter into a season of rest?

Sabbath Season

4. Do you have faith to take the steps to enter into your Sabbath Season?

CONCLUSION

"Joshua also set up another pile of twelve stones in the middle of the Jordan, at the place where the priests who carried the Ark of the Covenant were standing. And they are there to this day" (Joshua 4:9, NLT).

After crossing the Jordan River into the Promised Land, the Israelites built a memorial stone to God. It was common practice, in the Old Testament, to build a memorial as a tribute to remember what God had done. This was to serve as a reminder for the Israelites and for future generations.

Joshua stated,

> In the future, when your children ask you, 'What do these stones mean?' tell them that the flow of the Jordan was cut off before the ark of the covenant of the Lord. When it crossed the Jordan, the waters of the Jordan were cut off. These stones are to be a memorial to the people of Israel forever (Joshua 4:6–7).

This symbolized the miraculous provisions of God, to lead and guide his people, as they transitioned from slavery to freedom.

Sabbath Season

My Memorial Stone

This book is my spiritual memorial stone to remember what God has done during my Sabbath Season. It is a reminder of what God is able to do when I am faithfully obedient to His plan for my life. We all talk about letting go and letting God, but the reality is that this is one of the hardest things we will ever do. We are all addicted to control. Controlling not only our lives, but some of us also struggle with controlling other people. Learning to live by faith and to trust in God requires complete surrender. Initially, this time of surrender felt impossible. I was overcome with anxiety as I tried to trust God. But the more I relied on God, the more He continued to demonstrate that He was able to meet all my needs. God has brought me out of emotional bondage into a place of spiritual freedom. He restored my relationship with my mother and taught me the meaning of forgiveness. My Sabbath Season allowed me to release the burden of being in control and needing to know the future. He removed the things that held me captive. I thank God for the difficult times. This may sound strange or maybe you can relate. But, I truly thank God for the challenges because He has used them to reveal Himself to me. I thank Him for my wilderness experience. Praise God for the wilderness, because it shapes our character and makes us grateful when we enter into our Promised Land. Although it was difficult, God taught me that He would always be by my side. Even in the darkest and loneliest

Conclusion

days, He promised to be with me. If you are facing your own wilderness experience, God has something amazing on the other side, if you believe and never, ever give up.

The process of writing and publishing this book has truly been a test of my faith and courage. He taught that my testimony is not my own, but in fact, it was all for His glory. The lessons that I've learned during this season are priceless, because they have solidified my faith and trust in the character of my God. On this journey, I made many mistakes and continue to struggle with doubt and fear. But even with all mistakes and struggles, God has become my most intimate and closest confidant. He is my friend and lover of my soul. I trust Him more than anything or anyone. My relationship with God is my most valuable possession because with Him, I have everything I need. After going through some of the darkest times in my life, I know that it was God who brought me through. This confidence and trust is the perspective through which I live my life.

A Gift from God

> 'The Lord your God will give you rest by giving you this land' (Joshua 1:13).

The Sabbath is a gift from God. He created this for His children and it is what keeps us faithful and grounded. God wants to give us the things He promises, by faith. However, if we are constantly in work mode, we will miss the blessings. When we operate by faith and allow God to give to us, we are resting in the promise of God. Allow God to give you His best, by taking advantage of this biblical principle.

God certainly balanced out this concept of rest and work. God clearly called us to work. This book is not a call for us to abandon work. In fact, if you have any questions about that read the Book of Proverbs. In Proverbs, He tells us to look at the ant for inspiration. The issue that I hope this book sheds light on is the fact that we need balance.

We are missing out on a wonderful spiritual blessing, which actually helps us work effectively. The gift of rest also makes sense when we are working in our calling. This is a time where we reconnect with our Maker and He whispers His plan for us. He fills us in order that we can give to others out of the bountiful blessings that we receive from God. We can find peace and rest in His love.

Sabbath Prayer

I want to conclude this book with a prayer. As I share my story, I pray that this encourages you to begin to dig deeper into the Word of God and continue to seek out His will for you no matter where you are in life. The Sabbath Season is such a special time, and it is available to everyone. The Sabbath was a part of God's original design, before sin ever entered the world. This was a part of the plan that God had for us from the very beginning, to set aside this special time to delight in Him. God is pleased when we, by faith, enter into this rest. I hope that you will begin your own journey to enter into the rest of God.

Conclusion

Dear Abba, Father:

Thank you for the opportunity to share my story with others. I pray that you will use it to reach the hearts of people who need to hear this message. Abba, you love us so much that you set aside a time for us to delight in you. You promise to bless us if we take this time and make it Holy. Help us Father to be obedient to the times when you call us to rest. Help us to listen to you. Help us to trust you. You know what is best for us and you know what we need. Please increase our faith and help us to take the time to hear your voice. God we want to live for you, we want to please you. Give us the courage to truly take the time to rest, heal, and forgive.

We love you, Father.

I pray all this in Jesus' Name.

Amen.

Sabbath Season

Sabbath Reflection

Finally, will you open your heart and pray about your own journey to enter into His rest? (Write out your prayer here.)

_____
_____
_____
_____
_____
_____
_____
_____
_____
_____
_____
_____
_____
_____
_____
_____
_____
_____
_____
_____
_____
_____
_____

Conclusion

REFERENCES

Center for Disease Control. 2014. Insufficient Sleep Is a Public Health Epidemic. (Last Modified January 14, 2014). http://www.cdc.gov/features/dssleep/ (assessed January 16, 2014).

Harvard Medical Publication. 2004. Power of Forgiveness-Forgive Others. http://www.health.harvard.edu/press_releases/power_of_forgiveness (accessed January 16, 2014).

National Sleep Foundation. 2014. Facts or Stats. http://drowsydriving.org/about/facts- and-stats/ (accessed January 16, 2014).

RESOURCES

*I*n this book, I share about my abuse and I know many individuals experience some form of abuse in their life. I have included a few resources for anyone who may decide they want to reach out and talk to someone. There are often times other resources available at the state and local level in your community.

Rape, Abuse and Incest National Network (RAINN)
Hotline 1-800-656-HOPE (4673)
www.rainn.org

National Suicide Prevention Lifeline
Hotline 1-800-273-8255
www.suicidepreventionlife.org

Also, to learn more about Sabbath Season, visit our website for additional resources.
www.sabbathseason.com

Forgiveness was a big part of my journey. In addition to studying the scriptures and gaining a biblical conviction on forgiveness, I found the book *Forgiveness Diet* by Dr. Grady to be a great resource.
To learn more about forgiveness visit:
www.askdrgrady.com

ABOUT THE AUTHOR

Nichola Brown is a Licensed Clinical Social Worker (LICSW) in Washington, DC. Born in Montego Bay, Jamaica, Nichola has lived in the DC metropolitan area for most of her life. She has been a Mental Health Professional for several years and enjoys working with individuals and families. Nichola earned her Masters in Social Work from the University of Maryland-Baltimore, where she focused on Clinical Mental Health with a concentration in Employee Assistance Programs (EAP). She has worked in the private and public sector, where she has developed a passion for helping people find their calling.

Nichola believes in embracing the journey of life. Nichola credits her faith in God and seeking professional help, with overcoming her own trauma. She believes in the power of God to heal and also believes in the gift of Godly counsel to help people overcome the challenges of life. This is Nichola's first book and she is currently working on her next book.

If you would like to learn more about upcoming books and speaking events, follow her on Twitter and join her Facebook page.

Twitter @sabbathseason
Facebook fb/sabbathseason
Website www.sabbathseason.com

www.ingramcontent.com/pod-product-compliance
Lightning Source LLC
Chambersburg PA
CBHW020944090426
42736CB00010B/1254